Personal Finance Schooled

The Mandatory Class About Money, Investing, Budgeting, Saving & Passive Income

By: Christian Beach

information contained within this document, including, but not limited to, —errors, omissions, or inaccuracies.

Table of Contents

Introduction

Thank you for downloading my book: *"Personal Finance: Schooled - The Mandatory Class About Money, Investing, Budgeting, Saving & Passive Income."*

If you find yourself seeing other people accumulate wealth while you continue to struggle the same way you always have, this book is exactly what you need. This book is going to show you the difference in how wealthy and poor people think and how you can transform yourself from poor to wealth by making just a few simple changes.

Once you have seen the benefits that are gained when you change your habits and pay yourself first, you will wonder why no one told you these things before now. Each chapter in this book has been thoughtfully designed to help you learn a key point in personal finance and how you can best apply it to your life to reap the benefits, as well as teach you some of the common mistakes people make, as well as how you can avoid making the same mistakes.

Starting with what money is, as well as the differences between earning and making money, this book covers both basic and more in depth concepts in a way that will not leave you confused. Get ready to embark on a financial journey that is going to show you that there is no reason for you to live your life paycheck to paycheck. It is time for you to take control of your finances, learn to pay yourself first, and put yourself on the road to financial freedom.

Chapter 1: What Is Money? – Understanding The Consumer Society

Before we can dive into helping you learn how to become financially set and stable, or wealthy, we first need to understand what these words mean. What is money? Why is it important, and why do people never seem to have enough? In this chapter, we are going to answer these questions to enable you to have a clear understanding throughout the rest of this book. If you don't understand what money is and how it works, it is going to be increasingly difficult for you to get onto the road to financial freedom.

What Is Money?

When you hear the word money, you probably picture the bills and coins that are in your wallet. Or maybe you see your debit card, credit card or bills. All of these would be accurate. Money is defined as being any article or confirmable record that another will accept as compensation for products, services, or repayment of debts in a socio-economic context.

Money has four functions: a medium of exchange, a common measure of value, a standard of deferred payment, and a store of value. Below we are going to briefly look at what each of these means.

A Medium Of Exchange – This is when money is used to intermediate the exchange of goods and services. Money avoids the coincidence of wants problems and compares the value of dissimilar items.

A Common Measure Of Value – Money is a standard measure of and common denomination of trade. It is a basis of for quoting and bargaining of prices and is needed to develop efficient account systems.

A Standard Of Deferred Payment – This is an accepted way to settle a debt. When debts can be denominated in money, the real value of those debts can change due to inflation and deflation.

A Store Of Value – If money is to be a store of value, it has to be able to be saved, kept, and reclaimed in a reliable manner.

The value or worth of money has to also be persistently stable over time. By saving and storing money, you are enabling yourself to have purchasing power in the future.

Why Is Money Important?

While many people can agree that money is not everything in life, money does play a very important role in our lives. Obviously, we need money to provide our basic needs, a home, food, water and clothing. Beyond that, money is essential to help us achieve our life's goals and supports such as family, healthcare, education, charity, adventure and fun. Money also allows for us to have financial security. Having money means that you are not dependent on being employed, are not living paycheck to paycheck, and are not forced to put up with abuse from your boss because you need your job. When you have money, you are able to have more control over your life. You have the freedom to carve out your own path without the worries of being confined in a career where you are unhappy.
Many people imagine that to be wealthy, you need to live in the biggest house, drive the newest car and go on the most expensive vacations. However, that is not what this book, or what wealth is about. Having lots of money, or wealth is about having very few wants. It's about being able to make the choices that are best for you and your life without being limited or stressed out about still meeting your basic needs.

Why Do People Never Seem To Have Enough Money?

There are two main reasons that people never seem to have enough money and are always trying to become richer is because they are rich and not wealthy. While many people think that being rich and being wealthy are the same thing, they are very different. When you are wealthy, you aren't worried about money. You have enough money to meet your basic needs at all times. Someone who is wealthy is someone who is not going to face poverty. Someone who is rich is someone who has accumulated enough to purchase the comfort of a luxurious nature that is above the common people. However, many people who are rich, purchase these items using credit and are dependent on their jobs in order to make those payments. When you are rich, you are never really financially secure. Someone who is wealthy who is someone who is about to create a residual income stream. This means that they never have to work for their money, but they are always making money. People aim to become rich in life, as opposed to becoming wealthy.

What Is A Consumer Society?

The second big reason that people never seem to have enough money is that we live in a largely consumer based society. The main characteristic of a consumer based society is that the buying and selling of goods and services are the most important activity, both socially and economically. The more things that a person owns, the more successful they are deemed to be.

You can see examples of this all around you, here are a few examples of a consumer society you might find around you:

- Remember when you were in High School and really wanted that brand name binder, shoes, jacket, or sweater? Or in elementary school when you wanted to have a specific character on your lunch box? These are both examples of a consumer society. Here are two more examples:

- Neighbor One just bought a new car. It is a base model of an upscale brand and comes with a large price tag. When

Neighbor Two sees this, he decides that he also needs a new car. Instead of going for something that is realistically within his budget, he thinks of Neighbor One and decides to go with a higher end model of another upscale car brand. He makes sure that everyone who was excited for Neighbor One sees him park his new car outside his house;

- Family One just bought their family a new ten-foot pool for the backyard. Family Two lives next door. When they see Family One's new pool, they decide their eight-foot pool that they have owned for 3 years is no longer big enough for their family. They head out to the store and settle on a new twelve-foot pool.

In both of these examples, we can see where people are trying to one up each other. If you pay attention to the people around you, and maybe even yourself, you can see how the things you purchase become a large part of the conversations you have with one another, and how people almost compete to own the most things, the biggest things, or the most expensive things.

The consumer society that we live in is a huge part of why people aim to be rich instead of wanting to be wealthy. When you are wealthy, you aren't aiming to own more things. Instead, you are happy with the things you have and simply want to maintain your lifestyle.

The Value of a Dollar

When you have money, it can be hard to remember the value of a dollar. This is even more true in a consumer society. When people are making the choice to have the newest smart phone, nicest car, and biggest pool, they forget what the value of that money is.

To help you learn what the value of a dollar is, think of the time value that is associated with that money. If you are going to spend two hundred dollars on a smart phone, think about how many hours you needed to work to afford that phone. Ask yourself if that purchase is still worth it. You are likely going to find as you convert your purchases and expenses into the number of hours you are working to earn that money, you are going to spend less money on things you don't need. This is going to help you veer away from the consumer society most people live in.

Now that we have a good understanding of what money is, how it works, its value and the importance of money in our lives, we are going to look at some of the differences between making money and earning money, which are not the same thing.

Chapter 2: Earning Money And Making Money – What Is The Difference?

Many people think that earning money and making money are the same thing, but like with most opinions about money, this isn't the case. In this chapter, we are going to look at what it means to earn money and what it means to make money. We are also going to look at which of these categories most people fall under and why making money is better for you than earning money.

Earning Money

When you are earning money, you are trading your time and energy for money. In other words, you work for an hour, and you are paid for an hour. If you do not work for that hour, you aren't paid. It doesn't matter if you are paid hourly, on a salary or commission. You are being paid by someone else in exchange for your time and energy. This means that you are relying on some other entity for the money that is going to support you and your lifestyle. Another aspect to earning money is that when you work for an hour, you are only going to be paid for that hour once. This is important to remember as we look into what it means to make money.

Making Money

When you are making money, you use your time and energy once and get paid over and over again. Making money allows you to be independent and doesn't require you to depend on someone else for the rest of your life.

People who earn money are often the ones who are in debt and are living paycheck to paycheck. Those who are making money are wealthy and have much more financial freedom.

The idea of putting your time and energy into something once and being paid for it over and over again may seem as though it is too good to be true. Here are a few examples of ways people make money:

- Coming up with an invention that they are able to sell to a person or company and receive an ongoing royalty;

- Writing a play that is licensed to a production company to turn into a movie or TV show;

- Investing in real estate properties and renting them out for more than the mortgage cost and other expenses;

- Investing in a parking lot and renting out the same spaces every day;

- Investing in dividend-producing stocks or other interest-producing financial instruments that pay out regularly.

This should give you an idea of the limitless possibilities that are out there for ways to do something one and be paid over and over again for it. Some people refer to this as passive income instead of earned income, but anyone who has invested in an income producing asset knows it is rarely completely passive. There is usually consistent work that is going to be involved in ensuring the asset contains to produce a regular income.

Do You Need To Earn Money To Make Money?

Some people believe that it takes money in order to make money. While this is true, it doesn't always have to be your money that you use in order to make money. You could be able to start making money right away if you are able to borrow the money by having Some people believe that it takes money in order to make money. While this is true, it doesn't always have to be your money that you use in order to make money. You could be able to start making money right away if you are able to borrow the money by having someone invest in your idea, or through a loan. This is referred to as leverage.

Leverage is when you are able to utilize other people's time, energy, and money to make you money. This could mean that you take your idea for a play to a play wright who hasn't been successful financially yet, and partnering with that person to get the play written. It could also be working with an investor to financially back your real estate deals when they don't have the time to find them, and you don't have the money to back them. The downfall to using leverage is that you aren't completely in control of the process. However, leverage is a great way to get your money making career started.

Sometimes it doesn't take much money to create an income producing asset. Occasionally things might just fall into place the way you need them to and allow you to begin making money.

Why Is The Difference Between Making And Earning Money Important?

Eventually, you are going to be making enough money that you are going to be able to support your chosen lifestyle. At this time, you could choose to stop earning money. In other words, you can stop working at your day job and rely only on your "passive" income to support yourself. Alternatively, you can continue earning money until you are able to support both your chosen lifestyle as well as contribute to charities or community projects.

Chapter 3: Why Do We Want To Be Wealthy?

The idea of being wealthy and not having to work probably sounds pretty appealing to most people. However, other people might be thinking, but why would I want to be wealthy? I like my job, and I am not living beyond my means, and I am earning more money than I need to survive. If this is the case for you, there are still lots of reasons that being wealthy is more beneficial to being rich, and of course, why it is much more beneficial to be wealthy than to be poor.

Freedom – When you are wealthy, you have the freedom to do what you want, when you want it. You aren't confined by being needing to be at work at a certain time, needing to meet deadlines, or putting in a certain number of hours at a job. If an opportunity comes up, you are able to take advantage of it without worrying about your finances.

Options – When you are wealthy, you are able to take advantage of opportunities that other people may not have the finances to. You are able to take your life in any direction you choose too. You can choose to invest in ideas that are high risk and be able to reap the benefits of those risks without worrying about the loss you might incur.

Choices – With all of the options you have, you are able to make choices. Unlike those who are limited by their finances, when you are wealthy, you are able to make virtually any choice you want to.

Relationships – People who are wealthy, network and build on relationships. If you have money, people are going to start coming to you with options to get the best deals, investments and opportunities.

Connections – People who are wealthy typically have mentors who are able to help them. With any goal that a wealthy person has, they are able to surround themselves with people who are experts to help them get the result they are trying to achieve.

Philanthropy – Most wealthy people want to give back. It is human nature for us to want to contribute to a better world. While you don't need to have money to be a philanthropist, when you have money you have the freedom to do a lot more for others than you can when you don't have money.

Health – People who have money usually have a trainer to help them keep physically fit. Since they have money, wealthy people also tend to eat a lot better than those who don't have money and are therefore able to keep themselves healthier. They are also not worried about medical expenses.

Resources – Resources are more readily available to those who are wealthy. Whether you want to have your child in a specific school, live in a desirable neighborhood, travel, or anything else, you have a better chance of accomplishing these things if you are wealthy.

Experiences – When people have wealth behind them, they are able to experience anything they want to. They can travel the world, have a collection, or take part in any hobby they desire to. Since they have wealth, they are also able to ensure that their children are able to get the experiences they feel are important for them. All of these things can be done without the need to worry about where the money is going to come from and how long it is going to take for them to save up this money.

A lot of these things aren't only available to those who are wealthy. In fact, many people who are not wealthy find ways to do a lot of the same things as wealthy people. However, there is one big difference between how those who are wealthy and those who are not wealthy do these things. That difference is that when someone who is not wealthy tries to do these things, there needs to be thought and planning and budgeting. Often it requires that a second, and even a third, job is found. It can also require fundraising and asking other people for help. When you are wealthy, you are able to do the things above without needing to worry about where the money is coming from

In the next chapters, we are going to look at some of the habits that wealthy people have, as well as those that poor people have. Pay attention while you are reading these lists, and see where your habits fall. If you aren't happy with where your habits fall, make a point of changing your habits to lead your life to where you want it.

Chapter 4: Habits of Wealthy People

Those who are wealthy have a set of habits that are unique to them.

Meditation – Many people who are wealthy attribute that wealth to meditating. When you meditate, you are taking care of your body and mind by helping you to relax and focus your mind.

Wake Up Early – There are many wealthy people who attribute their wealth to being early risers. When you get up early, you are able to start your day ahead of everyone else. This means that you can respond to others, exercise and find some personal time before the day gets hectic. Early risers also tend to be happier and more proactive.

Network – People who are wealthy realize the importance of networking. Research has shown that networking leads people to performing better as work and helps them to become more innovative.

Stay Busy – People who are wealthy are rarely idle. When they do find themselves with spare time, they use it to learn something or to stay active.

Can Say No – Wealthy people know when they should say no, and they don't feel like they need to say yes. They realize that saying no to negativity, extra work and time wasting activities will allow them to increase their productivity.

Read – Wealthy people prefer to read over watching TV. When they read, they choose to read to read for learning purposes rather than for entertaining purposes.

Make To-Do Lists – Wealthy people write out their to-do lists before they go to bed. This allows them to set their priorities for the next day. They number their lists to help them identify which tasks are the most important and help them to stay on track.

Set Goals – People who are wealthy, set goals and visualize their success. If you don't set a goal and visualize how you are going to get there, you are never going to get there.

Manage Their Money – Wealthy people are wealthy because they invest their money wisely, look for new opportunities, and set aside money for emergencies. They are generous and willing to help people who are in need.

Question Themselves – Creating wealth is about critical thinking. Wealthy people surround themselves with people who think differently than they do. This enables them to think outside the box and question their beliefs. Doing this brings new opportunities to them.

Outsource – In order to create wealth, you need to be effective at managing your time. On any given day, you are going to accumulate busy work. By being able to outsource the mundane, but important, daily tasks to other people you are going to be able to accomplish more.

Live Minimally – Wealthy people don't do without things. However, they have developed the habit of knowing what is essential and what is a luxury. They may indulge in a few items, such as a nice house or car or brand name clothes, but they do not purchase more than they need.

Learn Every Day – Prosperous people make a mindful effort to grow, learn, and appreciate something new every day. By being able to learn and understand the way things work and how people operate, you are better able to predict the actions and needs of others and profit from it when the opportunity presents itself.

Show Gratitude – When you constantly have people around you, being able to express sincere gratitude is a good way to ensure that people have good opinions of you. It is also a good idea to make a habit of thanking people with a gift or a card.

Meet New People – Many people are fearful of speaking in public. People who are wealthy overcome this fear by meeting someone new every day. By talking to someone new every day, you are helping to build the confidence you need to address a larger group of people.

Eat Healthy – People who are wealthy watch what they eat. They limit the amount of junk food they are consuming. They value their health and because of that, they have longer lifespans which open up more opportunities to earn more money. They also make it a priority to ensure that they are bringing healthy food into their homes, this way when they do feel like snacking, they can do so without indulging in foods that are unhealthy.

Exercise Regularly – Like with healthy eating, wealthy people always find time in their day to work out. Working out is known to relieve stress and also helps you to feel better about yourself. Making the time to work out shows that wealthy people find it important to make themselves a priority.

Give Back – Charity and philanthropy are common among those who are wealthy. Giving back to the community is an important characteristic among the wealthy, and this is shown throughout history from Nelson Rockefeller and Andrew Carnegie to Carlos Slim and Bill Gates.

Understand Passions – One thing many wealthy people do, is incorporate their passion into their job. They don't work at a job because it is a paycheck. They work at a job because they are passionate about it, or some aspect of it. This is what enables them to be willing to devote so much of their time to their work; they genuinely love what they are doing.

As you can see, people who are wealthy are very much in control of their time and habits. They don't spend a lot of time doing nothing, but they do make it a habit of taking care of themselves. In the next chapter, we are going to look at some habits of the poor.

Chapter 5: Habits Of Poor People

People who are poor, or are living paycheck to paycheck, have a set of habits that is common among them. These habits are very different than the habits that wealthy people live by. While some of them may seem as though you aren't able to control them, you are going to find that the habits that you have that are in this list can be easily modified to look more like the list of habits that wealthy people have that we looked at in the previous chapter.

Gambling Habits – Seventy-seven percent of people who are poor, or living paycheck to paycheck, play the lottery on a regular basis. Many people who are poor also gamble on sports. Many people think that gambling is going to give them their big break into the world of the wealthy. However, gambling is not a sound plan. People who gamble are relying on random luck. The odds of winning Powerball, for example, are one in 175 million. That is virtually zero percent.

This means that people who are already living poor are spending money they can't afford on a very miniscule chance that they *might* win money. Many people might win a couple dollars, and maybe even a couple hundred or a couple thousand. The people that do win money, often put that money back into gambling, hoping it is going to pay off, and they are going to make even more money. However, this isn't how gambling works, as we stated before, gambling relies on random luck.

Time-Wasting Habits – Poor people tend to rely on one stream of income. They don't invest their time into building their careers or building a side business to generate more income. They leave work at work and home at home. Instead of spending their time finding ways to turn their passions into income, poor people tend to spend their time watching TV, surfing the internet, and reading for entertainment. When you spend all of your time watching TV, indulging in social media and surfing the internet, you are putting yourself in a position where you are constantly seeing ads that are prompting you to buy something that you don't need. You are seeing what all of your friends are doing and feel the need to spend money to keep up with them. Essentially, you are falling into the trap of our consumer society.

Time is money. When all of your time is spent on entertaining yourself, you aren't putting yourself in a position of making more money. Instead, you are putting yourself in a position of continuing to live your life the way you are at this moment. Time doesn't discriminate. There are twenty-four hours in a day, regardless of how much money you make. It's what you choose to do with that time that matters.

Bad Spending Habits – People who are poor don't tend to budget their money or track their spending. Poor people also tend to make spontaneous purchases and have a hard time being frugal. When you are making purchases without planning, you are often required to rely on credit cards. Many people who are poor have multiple credit cards, which people who are wealthy typically only have one.

Most people who fall into the category of poor, don't know where their money geos each month and are good at convincing themselves they need something. Many of these people have simply never been taught how to budget and why the value of a dollar is important.

Another habit of poor people is to rent their homes. When you don't own your home, you are unable to build home equity. Home equity comes in handy when you are going to retire or want to help your kids go to college.

Poor Saving Habits – Many people who are poor do not save money, and when they do, they aren't saving much. This means that when there is an unexpected cost, they are forced to rely on credit or, if there is no credit available, they take from one bill to pay for another. This creates a vicious circle of never getting ahead. People who are wealthy save twenty percent or more of their income.

You aren't going to be able to change your habits overnight. In fact, the average millionaire took thirty-two years to become wealthy. You can't change a few of your habits and expect to become wealthy instantly. It takes time and patience. In the next chapter, we are going to look into what it is going to take for you to become wealthy.

Chapter 6: Patience – Becoming Wealthy Does Not Happen Overnight

In the last two chapters, we looked at some of the habits wealthy people have compared to the habits that poor people have. This is not to imply that you can simply decide to change your habits and tomorrow you are going to wake up wealthy. It is going to take a lot more time and patience than that. It is also going to take a lot of hard work and commitment. However, it is not impossible.

Patience is easily one of the most important factors when it comes to money. While patience isn't a guarantee of success, it does dramatically increase your odds of success. Patience is also one of the hardest traits to learn. Especially since we live in a culture of now. We tend to look for instant gratification, and we are constantly bombarded by messages that are trying to convince us that this is okay. The messages we are seeing are telling us to buy now, to spend now, and to get what we want right now.

When you buy something now, instead of waiting until you can truly afford it, you cost yourself more money. This is because you are likely relying on credit to purchase the item that you want right now. Patience is the key to overcoming this.
Below we are going to look at a few of the ways patience is going to help you achieve your financial goals.

Patience Lets Your Money Grow – The longer you can hold onto your money, the more of it you are going to have. When you leave a pool of money alone, it can compound interest and grow before your eyes. This is going to allow you to afford more in the future, by being patient now.

Patience Teaches Your Discipline – When you find something that you want to have now, wait thirty days before you buy it. In many cases, you are going to find that you can live without the item that seemed so urgent just a few weeks ago. You are going to feel better about yourself because you were able to exercise discipline and aren't going to have buyer's remorse over the product you bought. Patience is going to help you to prevent mistakes from happening.

Patience Allows You To Seize Opportunities – By having the patience to wait instead of buying the item you want right now, you are going to be able to spend time comparison shopping and researching cheaper alternatives. If you aren't in a rush for an item, you can practice predatory shopping. Predatory shopping means that you watch and wait for bargains and markdowns which allow you to save even more money.

Patience Lets You Discover What's Important – As you age and mature, your values are going to change. If you are willing to wait, you are going to learn more about yourself and what is truly important to you. Patience is going to help you practice conscious spending and keep you from buying something that you aren't going to care to have in a few months.

Patience Keeps You Sane – Being patient means that you aren't going to care about having to keep up with other people on having what is new. It means that you are not going to give into fads and trends. You are going to be willing to buy last year's model of a product and keep it until it dies. It means you aren't going to care about what your neighbors have, and you are going to live a quiet and content life.

Being patient is going to lead you to be happier and lead you to wealth. It is hard to be patient when you are always watching TV, listening to the radio and using the internet. Our society doesn't believe in or encourage, patience. Our society is all about now and instant gratification. This is where practicing more of the habits that wealthy people practice is going to help you achieve your goals.

Another advantage of being patient is that you are going to be able to stay committed to your goals. If you aren't able to exercise patience you are going to have a hard time making a goal and seeing it through to the end. This means that when you make a goal to create and stick to a budget, which we are going to cover in the next chapter, you aren't going to have the patience to stick to the budget you created and followed it.

Chapter 7: Making a Budget, and Sticking To It

In theory, making a budget might seem incredibly simple. Or the idea of a budget might leave you confused and frustrated. In reality, creating a budget can be confusing and frustrating, but it can also be incredibly simple. In this chapter, we are going to outline the steps on how to create a budget as well as cover some tips to help you stick to your budget successfully.

What Is A Budget?

Before we get into how you to make a budget and how to use it, we are first going to look at what a budget is.

A budget is a written document or electronic file that is going to help you to take control of your personal finances. A budget is an excellent tool to help you manage your money and achieve your financial goals. A budget is a good idea for you if:

- You find that money is always tight;
- You aren't sure where your money is going;
- You are having a hard time paying off your debt;
- You don't save regularly; and
- You want to find ways to make your money stretch further.

A budget is going to give you a clear view on how much money you are bringing in, how much you are spending and how much you are saving. Creating a budget can help your find ways to eliminate your debt, reduce your spending, and have more money for the things that are really important to you.

Before You Begin Making A Budget

Before you start creating your budget, it is important that you know what your goals are as well as where your money is currently going.

Think About Your Goals – Take some time to think about what the goal of your budget it. Decide if you are trying to pay off your debts, have more money available, save for something, build a nest egg, go back to school. Your goal is yours individually, but it is important to have a goal in mind before you begin to create your budget.

Keep Track Of Your Money – Most people know how much money they make. However, what most people don't know, is where their money goes. Before you start making a budget, start tracking where your money is going. For one or two months, keep track of everything you purchase, from groceries to coffee. Keep a copy of all of your bills that you pay, and write it all down in a notebook. Doing this is going to help you understand your spending habits and put you on the path to success with your budget.

Making Your Budget

When you are ready to create your budget, you are going to follow four steps.

1. *Calculate Expenses* – The first thing you are going to need to do is calculate what your expenses are. You can use your bank statements, as well as the tracking you have already done to ensure that you are getting a clear picture. Since some things only happen every few months, or even once a year, it is important to go back through your records and make sure that you are accounting for everything. When you come to an expense that doesn't occur every month,

take the cost of that expense and divide it by twelve so you can see your average monthly expenses.

Keep in mind that it is imperative that you are thorough when you are adding up your expenses. A forgotten bill is going to throw off your budget when it crops up. A good rule of thumb is to add an addition ten to fifteen percent into your expenses over what you have calculated. This means that if you determined that you spend $1,500 a month, add $150 to $225 to that number.

2. *Determine Your Income* – Once you know what your expenses are, you are going to need to know what your actual income is. While you probably know what your salary is, you will get a more accurate picture by calculating any extra income as well. This can include cash gifts, alimony, child support, interest, and rental income.

3. *Figure Out What's Left* – Once you know your income and your expenses, you are going to be able to know if you have money left over, or if you are overspending.
   If you have money left over, congratulations. You can now earmark this money for savings or pay off debt. If you find that you are spending more than you are making, it is time to make some cuts so you can save money and not go further into debt. This is where tracking your spending will come in handy. If you find that you are spending two dollars a day on coffee, this works out to fourteen dollars a week and seven hundred and twenty-eight dollars a year. This is significant when you are looking at ways to cut your spending. If you aren't able to cut enough of your spending, you should consider ways that you can increase your income.

4. *Be Realistic* – When you are making your budget, be realistic with your numbers. Don't say that you are going to spend half of what you are going to spend on something. Doing this is only going to cause frustration when you are trying to stick to your budget. Be honest with yourself about where your money is going and what expenses you can cut.

Sticking To Your Budget

Making your budget is easier than it is going to be to successfully stick to it. While it is okay to fall off your budget once in a while, you want to make sure that this is the exception and not the rule. Below we are going to look at some tips on how you can be more successful at sticking to your budget.

Don't Carry Your Credit Cards Around – Availability is your enemy. If you are carrying your credit cards around, you are more likely to make an impulse purchase. This includes deleting your credit card information from your favorite websites.

Use Cash Only – When you are using cash to make purchases, you are far more aware of what you are spending. If you stick to using cash for all of your purchases, you can see when your money is gone. When your money is gone, you are stuck until your next budget cycle. This is going to lead to you being conscious of your spending choices, as you aren't going to want to leave yourself with no money to buy food.

Schedule A Budget Evaluation – Make time to sit down and look at your budget every couple of months. Your life is always changing and over time you might find that there are aspects of your budget that just don't work. Maybe you are making more or less money, or maybe your family has grown. Either way, it is your budget, and it is important that is works for you. Just don't lose sight of what your long term goals are.

Keep Track Of Your Money – Keep track of where you are spending your money. If you are finding that you aren't able to buy a number of groceries that you were expecting to, look at where you spent your money and what you spend it on. Knowing exactly where your money is going will make it easier for you to correct your budget and make it work for you.

Your budget doesn't need to be incredibly challenging. With a little patience and consistency, you will soon be sticking to your budget, and even find that you are coming in under budget some months.

Chapter 8: Paying Yourself First – What Does It Mean And Why Is It Important

Paying yourself first is incredibly important. However, many people misinterpret what this means. To some people, paying yourself first means that you buy yourself that big TV, ordering in dinner, or get new clothes. In fact, for many people, this is what they are being taught it means when they hear the phrase "pay yourself first." However, this is not what it means when you are advised to pay yourself first.

Paying yourself first means that you are putting money into your savings before you do anything else. Instead of paying all of your bills and expenses and then setting aside the rest, you first put your money into your savings and then you pay your bills and expenses.

This means that whatever amount you decided was going to go to your savings from your budget; that goes into savings first. Most people look at their savings as being optional. If you want to become wealthy, you need to stop looking at it that way. You need to make sure that you are paying yourself first.

Advantages to Paying Yourself First

When you pay yourself first, you are guaranteeing that you are going to have a nest egg to secure your future. This is also going to create a cushion for unexpected financial emergencies, such as your car breaking down, or unexpected medical expenses.

There is also a psychological benefit to paying yourself first. As you build savings, you can motivate yourself to save even more. This is because you are telling yourself that your future is the most important thing to you and not the cable company. While we all know that money cannot buy happiness, it can provide you with peace of mind.

As a final bonus, paying yourself first encourages sound fiscal habits. By making your savings the most important, instead of spending, you are going to have a better grasp on the role of opportunity costs and how they affect your choices.

Leave Your Savings Alone

Once you have saved up some money by paying yourself first, you might find yourself tempted to spend that money. Just because the money is in your savings account, that doesn't mean that you should spend it as soon as an opportunity presents itself. Here are a few tips on how you can prevent yourself from spending your savings money.

Know Why You Are Saving – If you are saving money for winter tires in six months, make sure you have consciously acknowledged that. The same holds true if you are saving for a trip, emergencies, vet bills, the list goes on. If you have more than one reason for saving money, create more than one savings account and separate your savings accordingly. Understanding why you are motivated to begin saving, you are less likely to decide you want something and raid your savings account.

Make Your Savings Hard To Access –As your savings account grows, it becomes easier and easier to justify taking a little bit of money out of those accounts to cover the expense of something you want. One way to avoid this is to put the accounts out of sight and out of mind. This can mean creating an account that you need to go into the bank to use the money, it can mean giving someone else the debit card to that account, and it can even mean putting them into a bank that you don't normally use.

Have Spendable Savings – Even though your savings might be earmarked for something that is really important to you, there might still come a time when you need to access the money. This is where your spendable savings comes in. While it may seem impossible to add another savings goal, it'll be far easier to save your savings if you have a stash of cash that you are allowed to spend.

Chapter 9: Common Financial Mistakes And How To Avoid Them

Now that you have a good idea on how to create a budget and why it is important to save, we are going to look at some of the most common financial mistakes, and how you can avoid them. Some of them were covered in previous chapters, but this chapter will look at each of these in a little more depth and help you to avoid making these mistakes and put you on the path towards becoming wealthy and financially free.

Failing To Plan – If you have a financial goal, and no plan on how you are going to reach that goal, you are never going to reach it. Failing to plan is planning to fail. Once you know what your financial goals are, create a plan to help you get there.

Passing On Company Plans – Many companies have health care plans and retirement plans. These plans are valuable benefits and are worth the monthly cost, especially since the money comes right off your paycheck. The amount of time it takes to enroll in these plans is a small investment that is worth it.

Not Planning For Retirement – Retirement isn't a pipe dream. It is a real event that you should plan for. It is never too early to begin saving for retirement. In fact, the longer you put off saving, the less you are going to have when you retire.

Not Creating A Budget – When you don't have a budget, you don't know where your money is going. As we covered before, small expenses add up. A budget helps to ensure that your money is all going to where it has been allocated and that you aren't overspending on things you don't need and that you don't forget to pay yourself.

Not Reviewing Statements – Once you have begun saving and investing, it is important to take the time to review what your money is doing. You might want to move your money around as time passes, and knowing what your money is doing will help you ensure you are on track to meet your financial goals.

Not Talking About Finances – Discussing finances with your partner is essential to make sure that you are both on the same page with your spending. Understanding one another's priorities and being able to develop strategies you can both agree on is essential to a successful relationship. It is also important that you teach your children about finances and money to ensure that they are on a good path when they reach adulthood.

Not Having Life Insurance – Many people believe they cannot afford life insurance. If you are working, your ability to earn money is a valuable asset to your family that should be protected. That's where life insurance comes in. In most cases, life insurance is less expensive than you think it is.

Not Having An Emergency Fund – If you don't have three to six months of living expenses saved up, now is a good time to begin working towards that goal. Credit cards are not a good fallback plan because it is going to cost you high-interest rates when you can't afford to pay them, it is also going to have a negative effect on your credit score. There is also the potential of your credit card not having enough money on it to cover the emergency.

Only Paying The Minimum On Debts – When you are only paying the minimum on your credit card and student loan debt, you are going to be paying them off for a long time. Even if you can only add a few dollars onto the payments each month, it is lowering the balance and therefore also lowering the amount of interest you are being charged on those debts.

Spending Money Frivolously – Great fortunes are usually lost one dollar at a time. While it may not seem like a big deal to have dinner out, or order a movie all of the little items, slowly add up. Just $25 a week on eating out ends up costing $1,300 per year. If you are currently experiencing financial hardship, avoiding this mistake matters.

Living On Borrowed Money – When you are relying on your credit card to get you through each month, you are slowly sinking yourself further and further into debt. When you use your credit card to purchase essential items, you are paying double digit interest rates on those purchases, which is making those things a lot more expensive.

Buying A New Car – For most people, when they get a car, they don't have the ability to pay for the car in cash. This means that they can't afford that new car. By borrowing money to buy a car, the consumer is paying interest on a depreciating asset, which only amplifies the difference between the value of the car and the price that is being paid for it. To make it worse, people tend to trade in their cars every few years and lose even more money on the trade. If you do need to take out a loan to pay for a vehicle, choose a vehicle that uses less gas, and costs less to insure and maintain.

Buying Too Much House – Many people think that bigger is better when it comes to a house, but that is not always a case. Unless you have a really large family, a bigger house is only going to end up costing you more in taxes, maintenance and utilities. When you purchase a house, purchase a house that meets your needs and doesn't grossly exceed them.

Living Paycheck To Paycheck – When you are living paycheck to paycheck, you are in a very precarious position. You are left needing every dime you earn, if you get sick and miss work, or lose a paycheck for any reasons, the results are disastrous. When you make savings a priority, you are no longer living paycheck to paycheck, and you always have a back-up plan should something happen to you, which means that you aren't going to be relying on credit.

By avoiding some of these common mistakes, you are going to be able to ensure that you are setting yourself up to succeed financially and putting yourself on the right path towards wealth and financial freedom. The best and easiest way to avoid making these mistakes is simply knowing that they happen. Being educated on what to avoid, instead of what to do helps many people avoid repeating common mistakes.

Chapter 10: Passive Income - What Is It, and How to Make It Work For You

As we've mentioned in Chapter 2, 'passive income' is another way of making money. When we think about making money, often our thoughts turn to what's called 'earned income.' Earned income is when you are actively going to work earning money – the key word is active, here: you perform a task, then you get paid for it. When you don't perform the task, the pay stops coming in. Most jobs that require you to work a 9 to 5 schedule, or involve commissions and quotas, might be considered types of 'earned income.'

Why Is Passive Income Important?

We all want to make more money. But whenever someone mentions that they need additional income, the traditional, very well-meaning, but stereotypical suggestion offered tends to boil down to "get a part-time job." The trouble is, not everyone has that luxury of time, let alone the energy reserves to put in all those extra hours. That's where passive income comes in.

In its simplest definition, passive income is a way to make money with very little investment of resources, be they monetary, or resources in the form of time and effort. A great benefit to making a little extra cash through passive income is that it'll help you pay off debt quickly. When you put an honest effort into something once, and then get paid for it over and over again, that's also considered earning a passive income. It might surprise you to know that, yes, there are indeed ways to make money without actively working for each and every paycheck.

Of course, the key word here is 'passive': you'll want to find ways you can make money without needing to do a task over and over again. At least, that's how it works in theory.

In reality, all sources of passive income do require some contribution of time and effort. But where passive income differs from regular earned income is in the amount of work required to make money. While some work is always required to make money, when you're making passive income, the amount of work you put in tends to be a lot less than when you're working for an earned income. Depending on the type of passive income you're generating, the time and effort you should need to put in will vary substantially. It could be as simple as making a few phone calls, logging into a few websites, checking your e-mail or participating in online discussions or teleconferencing a few times each week, or it could be more involved. Passive income is important in generating wealth because it is a way of making money for little effort.

As we've discussed, here are a variety ways people have successfully generated passive income:

- Coming up with an invention, brand, or intellectual property that you are able to sell for an ongoing royalty each time it is used commercially.
- Writing a book or stage production that is then licensed to a production company which adapts it into a movie or TV show, which then pays you a part of the proceeds from airings and ticket shows.
- Investing in a parking lot, and generating revenue from renting out the same parking spaces every day.
- Investing in stocks that produce stocks, or institutions and financial instruments that generate interest that pays out regularly.

Here are some other ideas for ways of generating passive income on a small budget:

Getting cashback rewards from credit cards – Cashback rewards might not seem like passive income, but when you think about it, it fits the description to a tee: you're getting money back, thereby making money, from doing nothing much else than swiping your credit card. And if you're already using a credit card to pay for some of your day to day purchases, you might as well be making money when you spend money. In this competitive market, many top rewards cards will let you earn anywhere from 1 to 5% cash back on the money you spend, with almost no additional effort on your part – all you need to do is swipe your credit card to pay for purchases. Even if you happen to be fairly frugal with your spending, you should endeavor to feel confident paying for your regular bills, groceries, gas, insurance, and all other expenses on credit. As your expenses add up, so too will your cashback rewards, essentially earning you money for doing absolutely nothing extra than simply spending money on things you'd be spending money on anyway. And if you love to travel and travel often, definitely check out the bonus offers being offered on many travel rewards credit cards; taking advantage of these could save you up to thousands of dollars on travel tickets and related purchases every year. It pays to investigate the deals available from the leading credit card companies in your area; you could stand to score big.

Investing in index funds – Index funds are a type of mutual fund that enables you to invest in the stock market in ways that are completely passive. But how does it do this? First of all, in order to really wrap our minds around what an index fund is, we need to know what a stock market index is. A stock market index is a number that indicates how much value is attributed to a group of stocks. As the value of this group of stocks changes, so does its index number in the stock market. If you've watched or even listened to the business segments of the evening news, chances are you've heard about stock indexes before without realizing it. Two of the most frequently referenced stock market indexes are the S&P 500 and the Dow Jones. Each stock market index concerns itself with of different kinds of stocks, but both indexes perform essentially similar functions: they let people know how their individual stocks are performing, and how the market is performing as a whole. Make sense so far? Now, let's talk about index funds.

As I've said before, an index fund is a type of mutual fund, meaning it's comprised of money pooled from a group of investors. Index funds are typically equipped with a portfolio that's been created to match a particular stock index, like the S&P 500 or the Dow Jones Industrial. So, let's say you decide to buy an index fund with a portfolio that tracks the S&P 500.

That index fund will try to purchase stocks in the S&P 500 in the same proportions as they exist in the market, so that the performance of the index fund usually stays on par with the performance of the S&P 500. Index funds aren't just limited to tracking a specific stock market index; index funds can also be created that track a specific business sector, like technology or healthcare.

"All right," you might be thinking to yourself, "So what's the difference between index funds and mutual funds?" The biggest difference between index funds and traditional mutual funds is that mutual funds need to be actively managed; index funds are completely passive. Traditional mutual funds need to be handled by a fund manager who, using his professional knowledge and expertise, actively selects stocks and trades them, buying and selling at the right times in order to achieve the most money by 'beating' the market. Index funds, on the other hand, relies very little, or not at all, upon human beings to make the decisions on which stocks to include in a fund.

Instead, a computer tracks the market and makes decisions that balances and re-balances the funds as necessary, ensuring that it always matches, as closely as possible, the stock market index it's tracking. Now, you might be asking, "But how could that possibly make me any money? Don't investors make money by beating the stock market, instead of just going with the flow? Why would I want to put my money in an index fund as opposed to a mutual fund?" That's a great question, and one that we're going to answer in the next section.

Index funds are one of the most powerful sources of passive income you can invest in – Research shows that, in the long run, index funds outperform traditionally managed mutual funds. Even when held against the performance of well-managed and diversified mutual fund portfolios, index funds wind up being more productive in the long term. You might have heard of the practice of keeping a diversified portfolio: because you have such a diverse selection of stocks or bonds, if one sector tanks, you'll have other investments that will counter that loss. Even so, in 2012, only 39% of the best-managed and well-diversified mutual funds performed better than their benchmark. Given that some actively managed funds have the potential to outstrip the market during some years, these occurrences are the exception, rather than the norm. In the long term, traditional mutual funds are likely to underperform.

And the reason for that is simple: it's because we're only human, and it's hard for any human to keep winning on a consistent basis. It's difficult, perhaps even impossible, to pick winning stocks and time the market just right, no matter how many years of professional experience you have under your belt. The stock market is a fluid arena, with ever-fluctuating ups and downs. With index funds, you'll find that more than likely, you won't outperform the market, but you will never dramatically underperform it either. Chances are, you will achieve an average return. That might not seem very exciting or dramatic, but consider that, during a highly volatile market, being able to net just an 'average' return with an index fund is far more desirable than losing a lot of money on a mutual fund that dramatically underperforms. Being average, during these times, will actually put you on top. Now, this is not to say that will always make money, or you will never lose money by investing in index funds. Because index funds closely follow the trends of a particular stock index, their performance is highly dependent on the performance of that stock index, for that particular year. The trick and the key to success with index funds is to play the long game: if you keep investing in it, even during a bad spell, you will eventually see a return on your investment. Naturally, there are industry veterans who believe that index funds are by no means the only sensible way to invest, but even these veterans are convinced that index funds are a sound investment. By consistently investing in index funds, even when the market sours, you will do alright in the long run, because in the long run, markets might experience drops, but they will eventually heal and go up again.

You don't have to know much about investing – To really succeed in mutual funds, you need to commit to a significant investment in time and work. To put it bluntly, to even have a chance (not a guarantee, a chance) at outperforming the market, you need to get aggressive, you need to breathe, eat, sleep, and live investing. If that sounds like something you simply don't have the time or energy for, you're definitely not alone: many of us would much rather spend the time with our families, or working on our businesses and careers. Even if you leave your investing to a professional manager, you'd still need to spend a lot of time researching fund managers to find one with a proven track record of beating the market – and even then, there's no guarantee that this manager will be able to repeat his performance on a consistent basis, year after year, or even most years. By investing in index funds instead, you might be settling for average, but more than one index fund investor has seen how their consistent averages outperform professional stock pickers. Best of all, index funds require next to no effort on your part to make money; you don't even need to know much about investing or economics. All you need is the initial investment, and then the patience to stick it out for the long term. You'd be surprised at how slow and steady really does win the race.

Index funds pay you first – Index funds are a great way for beginning investors to get their feet wet, because getting started in investing in index funds requires not only very little work, but also very little money. How much could you stand to save?

Let's say you've invested in a traditional mutual fund. By some stroke of sheer brilliance and a lot of luck, you've won big, and your fund ends up matching or beating an index. You're looking forward to reviewing your payout, but then realize that you might lose a big chunk of that money in fees: that's huge, to the tune of up to 25% of your return investment huge. And that's hugely devastating.

With index funds, you'll never have to worry about losing exorbitant amounts of your return, because index funds pay you first. By that, we mean that by investing in index funds, you get to keep more of your money because of the following three reasons.

Index funds incur no, or very little, sales commissions – When purchasing an actively managed mutual fund, you should expect to pay a sales commission of 4-6% to the brokerage firm. So when you decide to invest $1,000 into an actively managed fund, you should expect to pay $40-$60 on top of that amount to the brokerage firm. The firms will tell you that the commission fees pays for the professional services and guidance you will be getting from the fund manager, but as we've covered above, professionalism and guidance won't guarantee you'll outperform the market. Still, $40-$60 might not seem like much, but it definitely adds up if you're making multiple purchases. On top of this fee, brokerage firms will also deduct what typically amounts to 1-2% of the balance of your funds for operating expenses; this pays for your fund manager's wages and other expenses. Again, an annual payment of 1% might not seem like much, but consider that you might be investing for upwards of 20 years or more, and the expenses begin adding up. Let's say, for example, you invest $10,000 in an actively managed mutual fund. The brokerage firm handling your investment charges a 1% annual expense ratio. Let's say your fund somehow manages to perform consistently well year after year, gaining 10% each year for 20 years. Your $10,000 investment will have grown into $67,275. However, because you had 1% deducted from your balance each of these 20 years, $11,175 of your return will have gone straight into your broker's pocket, and you would bring home only $56,100. 1% over 20 years might not look like much, but I bet $11,175 certainly does.

Index funds are managed by a computer, which is set to automatically balance and rebalance your portfolio so that it closely mirrors a particular stock market index. Thus, there's no need to pay so much extra for human "expertise" or "services". When paying to invest in a mutual fund, most of your money goes towards your investment, not to a broker who will, more than likely, wind up underperforming the market in the long run. Operating costs are also significantly lower; the expense ratios for most index funds are less than 0.5%, and some even go as low as 0.1-0.2%. If you had an expense ratio of 0.18% in the example above, you would have paid a meager $2,168 to cover operating expenses over 20 years. That's much less demoralizing than losing over $11k. Tax efficiency. Another advantage that index funds have over traditional mutual funds is that they are tax efficient. Any time you sell a stock that made a profit, that profit becomes taxable, unless the proceeds of the sale are being held in the form of tax-free retirement account.

If you're not careful, these taxes can take a hefty chunk out of your return investment. Traditional mutual funds rely on selling profitable stocks frequently. And each time stocks are sold, a taxable event is created. And guess who this taxable event gets passed to? Yes, it gets passed on to the investor, which in this case, means you. When it comes to investing index funds, there is generally very little buying and selling involved, so tax costs are reduced. Meaning, more of your money will make its way back to you, instead of government coffers.

How do I get started investing in index funds? – While index funds can be your most powerful source of passive income, you'll find yourself well-rewarded by putting at least a little bit of time and effort into researching the topic before diving in. There are numerous books out there (such as this one!) that will teach you the basics about index funds, along with tried and true strategies that will help you build your portfolio. You might also spend some time researching specific funds: many experts will suggest building a portfolio that consists of at least three different types of funds: a domestic total market index fund, an international total market index fund, and a bond total market index fund. When selecting your stocks and bonds, be aware that each has different costs and minimum prerequisites for investment. By spending a little time browsing through your selections, you're sure to find the ones that are right for your portfolio and investment needs.

Ultimately, you will want to ensure that your portfolio contains a mixture of domestic and international funds, as well as both stock and bond funds. In doing so, you will have created for yourself a solid beginner's portfolio that has a lot of diversity, without having to work too much. In fact, the three-fund type of portfolio has proven so popular and so easy to compile that it is frequently called the "lazy portfolio". And believe it or not, once you've created your portfolio and made your investments, all you need to do is sit back and let your index funds make money for you in a completely hands-free way, for many years down the line.

Invest in real estate – The practice of investing in real estate has boomed in popularity over the last 50 years and has become quite a popular investment vehicle. However, buying and owning real estate can be a lot more complicated than investing in stocks and bonds. As anyone who has dabbled in real estate could tell you, investing in property or land is at least a little bit of an active venture. Still, once your investment is established and fully rented, you don't need to put much additional effort into managing your property and keeping it in good performance. And making money from your rent, certainly, does not require much extra effort from you.

One of the more common types of real estate investment is in basic rental properties. A person buys a property, and rents it out to a tenant. The owner, the landlord, is responsible for covering the mortgage, taxes, and costs of maintaining the property. The renter pays money to the landlord to cover all the costs mentioned above. While some landlords may charge more to produce a monthly profit, the most common strategy is to exercise patience, and only charge just enough rent to cover the expenses until the mortgage has been paid off. At this point, you can look forward to the majority of the rent turning into well-deserved profit. Even better, the property may also have appreciated in value over the course of your mortgage. Should this happen, you'd essentially wind up with a far more lucrative property than what you'd been paying for, a definite win in any investor's book.

The loan pay down is another great benefit of investing in rental properties. In the process of purchasing the property, you might have had to take out a loan; in making their rent payments, your tenants, essentially, will be helping you pay off that loan. Once the mortgage on the property has been paid in full, you can expect your cash flow to skyrocket dramatically. At this point, many property investors find that their mediocre investment blossoms into a fully realized retirement program.

Practically, it won't take many paid-off properties to provide a stable, and mostly passive income and prosperous future for you and your family.

There are, of course, problems that could arise from what might seem like the ideal investment plan. You might run into a bad tenant who leaves the property in a state of disrepair, or, perhaps worse, you could end up with no tenant at all, leaving you with a negative monthly cash flow. This is where doing your research prior to deciding to invest in a rental property, and before taking on renters, pays off big bucks in the long run. You'll want to find not only the right renter but also the right property in an area where vacancy rates are low.

If you might feel overwhelmed by tackling the day to day nuances of property management, there are professional property managers out there who are happy to handle the day to day affairs for you; going rates are usually 10% of the monthly rent. Of course, that takes a slice out of your overall cash flow, but leaving the burdens of property management to a professional whom you trust can free up a lot more of your time, and make your income that much more passive.

There are also real estate investment groups, which are like property managers, but on a larger scale. Think of real estate investment groups like mutual funds for rental properties. Should you decide to own a rental property, but don't want the hassle of being a landlord, you could consider partnering with a real estate investment group. Typically, these groups will buy or build a set of apartments or condos, and then allow investors to buy them through the company. By buying one of these properties, you will have joined the group. As a single investor, you have the option of owning one or multiple units of living space, and that's about where your involvement ends: the company takes care of the maintenance, advertising for renters, and interviewing potential tenants. In exchange, the company, not unexpectedly, takes a percentage of the monthly rent. Like teaming up with a property manager, partnering with a real estate investment group is often a safe way to get into real estate investment, while generating a regular income that's almost completely passive.

Another way of generating passive income comes in the form of REITs, which stands for Real Estate Investment Trusts. A REIT is created when a corporation (also known as a 'trust') uses its investors' money to purchase and operate rent-earning income properties. Just like any stock, REITs are bought and sold on most major exchanges. How can you invest in REITs in ways that will make you money in the long run? To answer this question, we have to delve a little deeper into REITs. You see, I n order for a trust to maintain its status as a REIT, it must pay out 90% of its taxable profits in the forms of dividends; by doing this, REITs avoid paying more exorbitant amounts in corporate income tax, where a regular company would be taxed its profits and must then decide whether or not to distribute its remaining after-tax profits as dividends. A lot like dividend-paying stocks, REITs are a firm investment for stock market investors seeking a regular, passive income. With REITs, investors can get a foot in the door and begin looking into non-residential investments such as shopping centers and office buildings. Another advantage that REITs grant their investors is that their investment properties are what we call "liquid". In other words, you shouldn't need a realtor to help you cash out your investment, allowing you to get that much more money back.

Leverage. A little while back, we talked briefly about leverage as a form of other sources of money you could use to start up your investment. Leverage just so happens to be a very powerful advantage that real estate investors have that's not available to investors in the stock market. In the stock market, if you want to invest in a stock, it is expected that you pay the full value of the stock at the time you place the buy order. Even when you are buying on margin, the amount you can borrow for your initial investment is usually a lot less than with real estate. When looking to invest in real estate, most conventional mortgages only require 25% down – depending on where you live, there might even be many mortgage types that require as little as 5% down. This means you can claim ownership over, and control the entire property and its associated equity by paying only a fraction of the total value. Naturally, over time, your mortgage will eventually equal the total value of the house at the time you purchased it, but you don't have to pay this amount upfront. The moment you make your first mortgage payment, and the papers are signed, you are given full control over the property. This is the perk that makes investing in real estate so inviting to landlords and real estate flippers. By needing to pay only a fraction of the value of their property, they can afford to get a second mortgage on their own homes and put money down on two or three other properties. And once they've made these down payments, they will have wound up with full control over these assets even though they have only paid for only a minor part of the total value and can start making money right away via renting or waiting for an opportunity to sell for a profit.

We've only scratched the surface when it comes to investing in real estate as a source of passive income. When it comes to real estate, there are virtually countless other types of potential investments (each with varying degrees of passive income earning potential), but the bottom line is that no investment offers a 100% guarantee of profitability. As with any market venture, it pays in the long term to start off by 'front loading' your efforts: before diving in, do your research, make careful and informed decisions, and weigh the costs and benefits of your actions.

Ways to Generate Income Online

Become a referral source – No matter what services they provide, every small business relies heavily on referral sources. Bookkeepers, plumbers, electricians, roofers, landscapers, carpet cleaning services and other independent contractors depend on referrals not only to maintain sales, but to thrive. Consider keeping a list of small businesses in your community, and contacting the owners to see if they have any kind of marketing offers available for cash referrals. If so, be ready to refer their quality services to your coworkers, and your friends and family. For each referral, just by talking to people, you could be earning a fee.

And, if you happen to work at a company that offers referral bonuses for either new employees or new customers, you should definitely take advantage of the offer. You'll be earning easy money for virtually no extra effort on your behalf.

Online Sources of Passive Income

Depending on how tech savvy you are, you'd be surprised at how many opportunities there are to generate passive income on the Internet. While some of these ideas don't necessarily fall into the traditional definition of 'passive income' (though one could argue that these new and exciting ideas have very little to do with the word 'traditional', in itself!), they do allow you to generate income and wealth with very little effort and interaction on your behalf.

Make money doing online surveys – Believe it or not, companies are looking to pay you for taking the time to tell them about your products. They do this by providing online surveys that take little more effort than clicking or typing your answers to questions on your screen. When you complete a survey, you are often rewarded with website-specific credits that can be redeemed for a variety of prizes like discount coupons, vouchers, and gift cards. Some sites will even award you with cash paid to a Paypal account. Sound too good to be true? Well, in many cases, unfortunately, it is; online surveys were so popular that especially in recent years, they have become the source of many online scams. But, fret not, According to professional review sites, two of the few legitimate paid survey companies are InboxDollars and Ipsos Panel, accessible at www.inboxdollars.com and www.ipsospanel.com respectively. Both have been verified to pay out credits or cash as promised, and as of 2016 both have maintained A+ ratings with the Better Business Bureau. You shouldn't, however, to earn hundreds of dollars in side income from surveys – and any sites that claim otherwise are likely trying to scam you. I've heard that there are some top-end surveys that offer $90-$100 payouts, but take more than an hour to complete. These surveys are few and far between, however, so expect most of the surveys you'll be presented with to come in shorter lengths and payouts.

Most of these surveys pay only a buck or two, but since they take only 10 to 15 minutes, you can get into the habit of answering surveys while you're watching TV or browsing the web. The effort you are required to put in will be minimal, and the payouts will keep adding up.

Sell your own products and services on the internet – You'd be surprised at the things you can find online. From handcrafted scarves to silly cartoon beanies to designer cat toys to simple 2HB pencils etched with customized monograms, it seems like there's a demand for everything on the Internet, even (or perhaps especially) all sorts of things people don't realize they want or need. I've even seen a small group of people who will prank call a number of your choice, for $5 a call! When it comes to marketing a product or service online, the possibilities are endless.

If you have the technical know-how, you might think about setting up a dedicated website for a product or service. If you already have a personal webspace or blog, then you're halfway there. And if the thought of putting together and maintaining your own website seems like far too much work, you can always sell it through an affiliate service, such as a website or blogs related to your product or service. You might think you will never make as much selling things online as you would from a salaried job, but think again: more than one stay-at-home mom has not only supplemented, but outright eclipsed their former 9-5 salaries by running a successful online business.

Now, certainly, making and selling products or services online is not strictly passive, but it's definitely a lot more passive than needing to get up, shower, and endure the daily 8:00 AM commute to the office every morning. Among the many perks of working online is that you set your own hours, and can work in the comfort of your own home, in your pajamas if you so like. And from the successful online business owners that I've spoken to, that benefit alone makes working online more than worth the time and energy you'd put into it!

Make YouTube Videos – If you're comfortable chatting and being yourself in front of a camera, you could be suited for a passive income making career making YouTube videos. This is a venture that's been growing rapidly for the past few years: all sorts of people in a broad spectrum of backgrounds and age groups are creating videos in just about any area that interests them: guides and tutorials, opinion pieces, makeup and fashion, style guides, grammar and language learning, music, comedy, animation, arts and crafts, movie and product reviews, restaurant and bar hopping, food tastings and adventure travel – the sky's the limit. All you need to do is creature your video and upload it to YouTube; the website takes care of the rest and will help you get the word out and promote your video to a massive online audience. YouTube's services are absolutely free to use – but there's quite a bit of effort that goes into creating interesting, high- quality videos. How could you possibly make money off this venture?

If you've ever watched a video online, you've probably encountered at least one 10-20 second advertisement that plays just before, or sometimes in the middle of the video. These ads are usually put on by YouTube's partnership with

Google AdSense; whenever a viewer clicks on one of these ads, YouTube gets paid a fee from the advertiser, and a portion goes to the video's creator. Of course, you probably shouldn't start making videos expecting your first upload to make you an instant millionaire; but if you put the effort into creating fun, enjoyable and compelling videos, promoting them on social media, and then opting to monetize them using Google AdSense, you could stand to make a fair bit of passive income. The beauty of this venture lies in the fact that once your video has been uploaded, it becomes a completely hands-free source of passive cash flow. Every viewer that comes along and watches your video and clicks on the ads that show up will earn you money; a single click might only net you a cent or two, but if your channel winds up getting hundreds, or thousands of returning viewers, those cents will just keep piling up, and you'll keep generating passive income without even trying.

Buy a blog – Web analysts estimate that thousands of blogs are created every year, and just as many are abandoned sometime afterward. I can understand if you have reservations buying anything associated with the term 'abandoned,' but if you're unfamiliar with the blog market, you should be aware that buying an abandoned blog is nothing like buying an abandoned car rusting away in the elements. In fact, even with a new car, as soon as it's out of the factory, the car begins to devalue. A car that's been well and truly abandoned loses even more of its factory value as the elements, corrosion and vandalism take its toll. But the same isn't true for blogs. If a blog, during its glory days, was able to amass a reasonable audience producing a decent amount of web traffic, and thereby cash flow, it could very well still be generating traffic and revenue even though it's been abandoned.

The reason for this is because most blogs employ Google AdSense, which generates a monthly revenue stream based on ads that appear on the site courtesy of Google. Blogs, like almost every other online venture, relies on regular updates that add fresh new content to keep its audience engaged and coming back to click week after week. When a blog has been abandoned, it means that the owner has effectively given up on it; no new content is being added, and more than likely its old audience members have moved onto something else: but what persists is its ads, and its backlinks – that is, sites that had linked to this blog sometime in the past will still be linked to this blog. As well, the abandoned website may be part of an affiliate program. It is through these ways that an abandoned blog still generates traffic, and therefore revenue. These sources of revenue will become passive income sources, once the blog belongs to you.

Experts say that, typically, blogs usually sell for 24 times their monthly income. This means that a site that generates $250 a month can usually be purchased for no more than $3,000. In other words, by putting money down on a $3,000 investment, you could stand to make $1,500 per year in cash flow. With some luck and good timing, you might be able to purchase the site for less than the typical 24 month's earnings, especially if the owner of the website is particularly anxious to sell. Keep an eye out for sites with what's called "evergreen" content, content that will continue generating revenue even after the site has been abandoned, sometimes even for years.

Start up your own blog or website – If the thought of investing in a piece of online real estate sounds daunting, you can always start up your own blog or website instead. By populating your blog with regular updates and engaging content about almost anything that interests you, and then monetizing it through paid-per-click ads such as those available from Google Adsense, you will be building your own source of passive income that will last for a long time.

Teach an online course – Most people are passionate about something, and people who are passionate tend to become quite knowledgeable about their favorite areas of interest. In fact, some people become so well-versed in their area of expertise that they could be considered self-taught experts! If this describes you to a tee, then perhaps teaching an online course can be your best route to gaining a passive income.

There are a number of websites that are simple and easy to use that will help you produce and get your content in front of potential students. Courses often incorporate audio files for listening on the go, video lessons, checklists for completing learning goals you recommend in your video lessons, informative interviews, short self-published ebooks to supplement your courses, and more. You can even create several lesson packages at different price points, so interested students will be able to shop and purchase the lesson package that best fits their need and budget. It's definitely best practice to include a 'deluxe' or 'the works' package for the highest price point, then set lower price points for smaller packages. In this way, you maximize your audience and therefore the volume of orders, and your audience gets to maximize their value for their learning. Of course, the sites will take a part of the profits from each lesson you sell, but once your lessons have been uploaded, you'll be generating a steady influx of regular passive income each time they're downloaded.

Publish an online guide – If the thought of editing your own video or filming yourself in front of a camera makes you feel squirmy, you could go the route of publishing an online guide. Publishing an online guide is a lot like running your own website, only you aren't necessarily promoting a specific product, but are supplying as much information on an area of your expertise as possible. And, just as importantly, you are making this information visually appealing, and easily accessible to your audience. Perhaps you're making a guide to the best 'hidden' bed and breakfast spots in the United States: on your website, you will want to feature a map of the country, and allow someone to click on each state to see an overlay of the addresses, contact information, and your personal review of each venue. Avoid getting too wordy, and stick to providing specific information in an easily readable and visually attractive guide-like format that the typical user can peruse, be impressed by, and ultimately absorb in just a few minutes of light reading. As with other website suggestions, the passive income you will be making will come via advertisements through Google AdSense, affiliate links, and even special memberships for exclusive web content you can sell from your guide.

Become an Affiliate Marketer – Once you've gotten the hang of managing and developing blogs and running a bustling website for a while, you might think about reaching out to vendors and companies to establish a relationship as an affiliate marketer. Affiliate marketing is when you promote specific products or services on your site, for either a flat fee or the percentage of the amount of each sale completed. Affiliate marketing isn't as intimidating in practice as it might sound: many, many companies in the world are, after all, interested in selling their products to as many markets, and in as many places as they can. You can find a variety of merchants, vendors, and websites either by contacting the vendors and developers directly: for websites, look for an 'Affiliate' link. There are also websites that are dedicated to connecting vendors and affiliate marketers. Again, this works best after you've established an online presence via a high-traffic website or blog, and if the product or service you are wanting to affiliate with are ones that you are personally very interested in, and are highly relevant to the content of your website.

Profit from flipping domain names – You might not have heard of the term 'domain name', but if you've ever been on the internet, you've seen one. Domain names are the .coms, .orgs, .edus and more that you see on your address bars of your favorite web browser. And you might be surprised to know that there's a fair bit of profit to be had in the market of buying and selling domain names. Like its counterpart in real estate, 'flipping' domain names involves buying domain names and then selling them at a later date for a profit. But flipping properties requires a hefty investment of time, effort, and monetary resources in renovation costs and sweat equity; as far as real estate investments go, property flipping is long term, and could hardly be considered a passive way to earn an income. Thankfully, flipping domain names is very unlike its counterpart in real estate this way. Most of the work you should expect to do comes in the form of researching and compiling a list of domain names, making your purchases, and then later selling them. Like most investment ventures, especially if you're starting out with a small budget, more often than not it's best to buy lower cost domains and play the long game: that is, by generating small but frequent profits that will eventually add up over time. Many online marketplaces will specialize in buying or selling domain names, and some of these marketplaces you might even have already heard of: popular domain marketplaces include Ebay, Flippa, Sedo, and Godaddy.com.

In the heyday of the domain trade, it used to be that acquiring and selling an internet domain required a substantial amount of work from making adjustments to the HTML, integrating content, and manually transferring websites. Now, domain marketplaces make it easy to sort through lists of popular domains, bid on or purchase them outright, and later easily transfer them to other buyers. Most of the effort that is required from you is to locate domain names that are fun, make an impact or is otherwise appealing and attractive in some way.

Another benefit inherent to the practice of domain flipping is that it incurs low risk, and doesn't require a large starting budget to dabble in. Experts report that once you have set up a reliable system, the amount of work you should expect to put in amounts to no more than a few minutes to an hour of work each day. Sounds like a pretty good source of mostly-passive revenue to me!

Domain flipping is a lot like flipping websites, which we've discussed earlier. The key difference is that a domain does not necessarily have to have a website built on it: think of it like purchasing an empty plot of land with a mailing address, with no home yet built on it. It is empty real estate, and depending on the attractiveness of its address, can be loaded with potential.

Like websites, domain names that have been abandoned can still generate revenue. In fact, these domains typically fetch more lucrative prices names because they are considered 'aged.' The reason for this is because the longer a domain has been around on the Internet, the more search engines will have found and linked to it, and more than likely it will have aged out of what has been termed the 'Google Sandbox.' As well, for website and content developers, aged domains are attractive because they can lend both history and credibility to a website or other online endeavor, especially in niche markets.

There are many guides out there that will give you a thorough overview and many tips on the subtle, and not so subtle art of domain flipping. When picking domain names, you will most often want to stick to the mantra of "keep it simple, and keep it catchy": as well, experts suggest avoiding domain names with numbers or overly elaborate ways of spelling ordinary words. You want your domain name to be as marketable as it can be, and that includes marketing via word of mouth. Some of the most popular websites follow this rule: facebook.com, twitter.com, and google.com all have pithy, catchy names that are spelled pretty much like they sound. Let's face it: facebook would be a lot less marketable if it was located at www.f8zebook.com instead of www.facebook.com. Another thing you should be aware of is that domain marketplaces can be surprisingly active venues, so expect some competition from other buyers!

All in all, once you have gotten into the habit and developed a system for selecting profitable domain names and mastering the auction interfaces, you should expect to have to contribute little effort into making successful sales and enjoying the profits.

Set up a website selling a product– If you are planning on selling a product or service online, you might as well have a website for it. And if you have a website for it, you might as well be making money from the website as well. Dedicated websites can earn you a surprising amount of passive income if you decide to monetize it by running Google Adsense.

Do note that your website doesn't have to sell a product that you make yourself. As long as you're fairly knowledgeable about a product, you can dedicate your website to selling it. The monetizing techniques are similar to marketing a product that you create yourself; the only difference is that you won't have to worry about creating your own product, but familiarizing yourself with, and selling someone else's product.

If you decide you have a knack for making websites that promote goods and services, you may find that you're able to add other products that are related to the one you're promoting. The more products you are able to promote actively on a single website, the more traffic you will stand to gain, and the more traffic your website generates, the higher your passive revenue.

As with many of the online ventures we've described, setting up a website could hardly be considered a 100% passive effort. Purchasing a domain and getting a website up and running requires a generous degree of effort, but once it's been published and the appropriate monetization efforts set up, the time and energy you'd need to invest in the venture goes down, while your revenue goes up. As an added bonus, if you are able to arrange for the product to be shipped to customers directly from the manufacturer, that's another activity you can cross off your list and put more 'passive' into your passive income.

Make money by doing online tasks you'd do anyway – Some survey companies like InboxDollars and Ipsos Panel mentioned above, along with other reputable websites like

Swagbucks, will offer you more easy opportunities to make a few bucks, other than surveys. Most of these opportunities involve doing things you already do on a regular basis, like searching the web, shopping for products online, playing simple games on your computer, and more. By taking advantage of the rotating, often daily opportunities offered on these sites, you could pick up a little extra cash for doing what you already do online. Like the previous tip about online surveys, however, be sure you're only accepting these kinds of offers from sites you trust. If you're just starting out, it pays to do your research: browse for user reviews of these sites, and look them up on the Better Business Bureau to verify that they are the real deal.

Ways to generate Income without the Internet

Become a silent partner – If you know of a successful business that just happens to be in need of capital for an upcoming expansion, you might consider becoming an investor and providing that needed capital. However, instead of simply offering a loan to the business owner, you can treat this as a business opportunity and inquire about taking an equity position in the business. In this way, you will become an investor in the business; more specifically, you will have become a silent partner. A silent partner typically doesn't (and should not) have a role in the day to day operation of the business: that's where the term 'silent' comes in. You're leaving the day to day operations in the hands of the business owner, but you get to participate in a portion of the profits the business generates. As a silent partner, you're not going to be brought into a company because of your knowledge of the company's policy, best practices or operations; silent partners are brought in for their financial resources. As a silent partner at this point, your tasks as a business partner will chiefly be centered around managing your business finances, while keeping track of how your partner is handling the business's operations. It's because of the latter point that becoming a silent partner is not 100% a passive activity. However, it is mostly passive, because your partner will be handling the actual operation of the business. What you will have say in, however, is anything that affects the management of the company because, essentially, management and its choice of direction might be the reason for your partnership in the first place. The key to being a successful silent partner, and incidentally these initial steps are where most of your efforts will be focused on, is to do your due diligence in thoroughly evaluating all aspects of the company prior to committing to your investment. The onus will be on you to take responsibility of researching the company's history as well as its profit and loss statements and to evaluate the company's potential performance in the market of the future. The upside is that a specialized knowledge of investing, or of your company's operations, are not at all necessary to becoming a successful silent partner.

That said, you should be aware that the most important aspect of being a silent partner, according to the experts, is to agree upon a strict and well-detailed partnership agreement. And a key topic that this agreement should outline, in no uncertain terms, is the limits of involvement in your partnership agreement. It is also vital for a good partnership agreement to establish an exit strategy should the agreement move in a direction that neither party is happy with. This can be a buyout clause no part of the company, or some form of loss mitigation for you, the investor. This is crucial for both you and the company you intend to partner with. If and when problems arise, the market sours, or the company hits a rough spot, your partner company will have the security of knowing the limitations of their silent investor's involvement in their company, preventing potential disasters that could arise when panicking investors begin arguing with company managers over how best to fix the company's ailments. And you will know precisely how your investments can be protected should unexpected problems arise.

Apart from the initial commitment of capital and the establishment of a solid partnership agreement, you will need to place your trust (both psychological and monetary) in your partners to run the company's daily operations. Other than that, there is little other responsibility for a silent partner other than to participate in and enjoy the profits generated by the company, making silent partnerships a great way of earning passive income.

Install usage-gathering apps from reputable sources – There are a surprising number of reputable companies, including Google, that will pay you to install their app on your cell phone. Even better, they will keep paying you for every month the app remains installed on your cell phone. These apps normally collect data from your cell phone: which sites you're visiting, what games you are playing, what other apps you're downloading, what times of day you're browsing the internet, how often you stay on websites and use apps, and more. This data is used to help companies better understand how normal people – their clients – use the web and their mobile services. So it should come at no surprise that companies would actually turn to paying people for this knowledge. Think of it as a completely passive way of conducting ongoing product testing and reporting, and being paid for it. Naturally, in the untamed wilderness of the digital online world, there are many fakes and imitations out there, so be sure you are only signing up for apps being offered by major, trusted companies. Amazon, for example, has an app that pays a small amount each month to people who help contribute research about what they're buying online. Both iPhone and Android offer apps that track and monitor your phone usage and will pay you every month you have the app installed. Like online surveys, don't expect a big payout at the end of every month just from swiping to unlock your phone, making calls and browsing the web several times a day. But if you're not overly wary about the privacy of your phone use, these offers are great ways of establishing small, but regular and completely passive income sources.

Put your photography to work – Do you fancy yourself an amateur photographer? If you consider photography a serious enough hobby to have splurged on a fancy camera, you might be able to put your photos to work for you. Photography websites such as Shutterstock and iStockphoto can provide you with ways to monetize your photo uploads by selling your images as stock photos. Depending on the site, you will earn either a flat fee for each photo sold, or a percentage of your listed price. It's important to note that the websites themselves won't be the ones buying your photos from you. The websites act as simply the middlemen, offering you the venue, or the marketplace in which to sell your photos, and they keep a cut of the proceeds. The website will also handle all the technical details in transferring your images to your clients. In this way, a single photo could wind up generating steady passive income for you, in the sense that the same photo can be sold again and again. Many photography sites will require you to have a camera powerful enough to snap high-quality photos, and will only accept submissions that meet a certain megapixel count. Once your photos are submitted, be sure to market your images by assigning it relevant keywords, as these form the search terms with which potential buyers will be browsing when shopping for stock photos.

Rent out space in your home with Airbnb – If all this talk of programming, website development and digital content creation might be sending your mind into a tailspin, take a breather! While it helps to have some software and Internet savvy, not every source of passive income online has to be so demanding of such specific computer skills. Airbnb is one such example. If you've never heard of Airbnb, fear not: it's a web service that has only been around for a few years, and has only recently exploded in popularity across the globe. Airbnb is a service that allows people to rent their homes, or other residential spaces, to globetrotting travelers looking for temporary accommodations, but don't want to pay for the normally exorbitant prices for hotel rooms in the area. By signing up with Airbnb, you can effectively turn your residence into a powerful source of weekly passive income, just by renting out space to travelers. If you already have a space in your home dedicated to rentals, Airbnb can help you reach a global audience, as its online popularity will enable you to connect to potential renters year-round, no matter what part of the world they're traveling from. How much you could stand to make a will, of course, depend on various factors including the size and condition of your home, and its location in relation to popular travel destinations. If you happen to live in a high-cost city, or close to a popular resort, the income you should expect to generate from rentals will be much higher. With its worldwide reach and convenient advertising options, Airbnb is a great way to earn a passive income from a space in your home that would just be sitting empty for most of the year, otherwise.

Pay off a credit card bill – Pay off two! Out of all the creative and entrepreneurial ways of generating passive income we've gone over so far, the suggestion of paying off your credit card bills hardly seems like an exciting one. In fact, it might even seem hardly creative or entrepreneurial at all! But, let's try putting it in another way: the money that you owe in credit card balances every month is a fixed expense. And in strictly financial terms, reducing a fixed expense is the equivalent of creating passive income. You've probably heard the adage "a penny saved is a penny earned"; in the case of credit cards, the saying holds true, especially when you think about it this way: "paying off a penny owed is a penny earned". By paying off our credit card expenses in a timely fashion, you are saving yourself from having to pay hefty interest fees every month. And for every penny you do not have to pay in interest fees, that's a penny of passive income. For example, let's say you owe $10,000 on a credit card with a monthly payment of 2% of the balance, or $200 each month. Should you manage to pay the card off, you're freeing up $2,400 per year in cash flow that you would've otherwise spent on the interest on this card. In other words, that's like getting a guaranteed a 24% return on a $10,000 investment. Now, how's that for exciting?

Build an app – If we were to go back less than ten years ago, and few people would have even heard of the term 'app'. These days, there are apps for everything: timing your oven, monitoring your fitness levels and water intake, scheduling meetings, heck, there are even apps for scheduling your meeting schedules. And it's not that apps are merely saturating the market – there is a genuine demand for apps that fulfill many different needs. Many people – if not just about everyone – owns and uses a smartphone these days, and everyone who owns a smartphone downloads apps.

The fact is, apps make lives easier for many people. But with the proliferation of apps out there, the obvious question you might be asking yourself is this: how am I ever going to create something unique, that stands even a remote chance at competing in the market? Well, these are fair questions to ask but don' let them discourage you. Some of the best and most popular apps out there are born from fresh, creative ideas. If you can come up with something unique, you may well find that you can eke out your corner of the market. When it comes to apps, uniqueness and simplicity make a winning combination: the more useful your app and the simpler it is to use the broader your audience.

If you are familiar with how to code or are willing to learn, you're already well on your way to putting out your own app product. Otherwise, there is always the possibility of hiring a developer to build your app based on your idea. Do note that this can wind up being a very expensive option to start up, although more than likely your end product will be an exceptionally professional-looking app.

Once it's created and published on the online app store of your choice, you will be making passive income in the form of proceeds from each person who downloads your app. If you offer micro transactions or purchasable features from within the app, you can expect additional passive income from those sources as well.

Conclusion

Now that you know what money is, what wealth is and how you can attain wealth, you are ready to embark on your journey. Start by identifying which poor habits you have and change them into the habits that wealthy people have. Remember that you can't change your habits overnight. Take your time and change one thing at a time. If you try to change too much at a time you are going to feel frustrated.

Sit down and set yourself up with a realistic budget that you can stick to. Be patient with yourself if you break your budget a couple of times while you are adjusting to it. Adapt your budget as you have to, and before you know it, it will be second nature to you to stick to your budget.

The most important thing to take away from this book is to pay yourself first. When you aren't paying yourself first, you aren't going to get ahead. You need to tell yourself that your financial future is more important than anything else. The rest of your budget can be modified to make it fit your lifestyle if you need to. Paying yourself first is also important in helping you to learn to stick to your budget.

Knowing the tips in this book is only part of the answer to attaining wealth and financial freedom. Remember that you also need to be patient and committed to the process. Wealth is not going to come to you overnight, but with perseverance, you will soon worry less and less about more and be happier and find more joy in your life.

Thank you again for downloading my book. I hope this book was able to answer all of your financial questions and has given you the confidence to embark on your journey to financial freedom.

Made in the USA
Lexington, KY
08 February 2017